Ear And Ethos

by Leonard Schwartz

Poetry

Objects of Thought, Attempts at Speech (1990)
Exiles: Ends (1991)
Gnostic Blessing (1992)
Words Before The Articulate (1997)
The Tower of Diverse Shores (2003)
Ear and Ethos (2005)

Essays

A Flicker At The Edge of Things:
Essays Towards A Poetics (1998).

Co-editor

Primary Trouble: An Anthology of
Contemporary American Poetry (1996)
An Anthology of New (American) Poets (1998)
Crossing Centuries: The New Generation in Russian Poetry (2000)
Contemporary American Poetry (in Romanian) (2005)

Ear And Ethos:
New Poems

Leonard Schwartz

Talisman House, Publishers
Jersey City, New Jersey

Published in the United States of America by
Talisman House, Publishers
P.O. Box 3157
Jersey City, New Jersey 07303-3157

Manufactured in the United States of America
Printed on acid-free paper

ISBN: 1-58498-043-5

Acknowledgments

Some of these poems have appeared in *Arras*, *Ars Interpres*, *Conjunctions*, *Denver Quarterly*, *Fo Arm*, *Ideya*, *Luna*, *Salt*, *Sentence*, *Talisman*, *Tinfish*, *Titanic Operas*, *26*, *Vert*, *Verse*, and *W*. Many thanks to the editors of those publications.

For Cleo

Table of Contents

Transcendental Tabby: The Translation

"To say that the transcendental is historically constituted amounts to saying that universality cannot be assigned to it; it is necessary to think of a particular transcendental. But after all, there is nothing more mysterious than what is collectively called a culture." —Guy Lardeau, "L'histoire comme nuit de Walpurgis"

In such manner Guy Lardeau invites us to contemplate a contradiction – the particular transcendental. Contradiction, because one of the attributes of the transcendental is held to be its universal grounds. Contemplation, because that is what the mind does, at least one committed to both a cognitive process and a mode of thought that goes beyond the simply analytical. One concept that may occur to us here is "strategic transcendentalism": one holds a condition to be transcendental or necessary to perception itself for specific political or tactical purposes. Another phenomenon that may come to mind here is that of the lyric poem: the lyric poem is a construct capable of maintaining equilibrium among contradictions and as such is singly able to accommodate the needs of such a slippery imperative ("negative capability"). Surely the allure of the poem is partly this, and the concomitant promise of mystery without belief. Our texts are the living evidence of an ethics of ambiguity.

I positioned the transcendental lyric in like manner in my essay from the 1990's "A Flicker At The Edge Of Things." Things here – "here" variously meaning in what passes for my mind, the room in which I sit and write, America, the shifting continents – flicker, and poetry is still the flicker at the edge. Some edges are as eternal as the need for a center, others are as ephemeral as perspective. What the language needs at any given moment shifts. The more things change, the more things change. You can never put your river into the same flume twice, because that would already be water under the bridge, and so on and so forth. The transcendental signifier, floating downstream, over flumes and under bridges, is like the spindle or seed of some plant, waiting to be thrown to the bank by a particularly violent movement of the water, where it might take root. A fluid foundationalism is always sensitive.

Now the particularly violent movement that has provoked a literary imperative in its aftermath is the Western recoil against the Arab and Islamic worlds. "Orientalism," so utterly exploited by European colonial powers and so carefully dissected and exposed by the late Edward Said, finds a new bloom of its own in the Bush Administration's version of what we are at war against in the Islamic world. Paid pundits speak of a "clash of civilizations." The White Man's Burden, which was to civilize the native, is reconstituted as the necessity to bring democracy to those in the Middle East yet too primitive to know this sacred form of government. We know all too well what violence has been unleashed in our names on the basis of these and other related ideological precepts. At the edge of things we watch with horror, demonstrate with desperation, and write vociferously. In 2001 Andrew Joron wrote in his "The Emergency of Poetry": "What good is poetry at a time like this? It feels right to ask this question, and at the same time to resist the range of predictable answers, such as: Poetry is useless, therein lies its freedom. Or, poetry has the power to expose ideology; gives a voice to that which has been denied a voice; serves as a call to action; consoles and counsels; keeps the spirit alive." For Joron, none of these functions suffice. There is only one function that is efficacious. That is the lament. "The lament, no less than anger, refuses to accept the fact of suffering. But while anger must possess the stimulus of a proximate cause — or else it eventually fades away — the lament has a universal cause, and rises undiminished through millennia of cultural mediation. Unlike anger, the lament survives translation into silence, into ruins."

For me Joron's lament is resonant, at least of one phase of our writing under the current imperative. The other phase has involved a working with language that might undermine the nauseating dichotomies that underpin the justification of Empire, the clash of civilizations, and the erosion of civil liberties. Poetry is language, and in poetry false dichotomies can best be dissolved, since the false dichotomies themselves are only frozen language. In the "Apple Anyone Sonnets," I set out to write a series of poems using only English words derived from Arabic, or suspected of having such derivation. Later that seemed a further segregation, and I collaged those materials with Shakespeare cut ups and rewrites — the name

"Shakespeare" conjuring up the conservative pride and core of "English" — and I kept doing this until I had the "Apple Anyone Sonnets."

Languages are interdependent, as are cultures. The texture of one can be raised up and felt in another. Some of the words I used later were discovered to be of Persian origin, or of contested origin. (As for example the word "mulatto": of course the word "mulatto" would be of contested origin.) That isn't the point. The point is the one Lardeau makes: there is nothing more mysterious than what is collectively called a culture. Robert Duncan's observation (since confirmed by many medieval scholars) that the figure of Beatrice in Dante's Divine Comedy, presumably the very pinnacle of Christian literary art, is in fact drawn from Islamic Sufi sources, might also be offered as a particular material evidence of the strangely synthetic nature of all culture. Or else Ron Silliman, who writes: "the words are never our own. Rather, they are our own usages of a determinate coding passed down to us like all other products of civilization, organized into a single, capitalist, world economy. Questions of national language and those of genre parallel one another in that they primarily reflect positionality within the total, historical, social fact."

If it is a privilege to be able to allow one's brain to travel in thousands of directions all at once (and it is), then part of the responsibility of that privilege remains the imagination of positionality in relation to a proposed total grid, just as Silliman argues. Of course this move is dangerous, because it bears a structural resemblance to the imagination of Empire, in which all points are united or yoked into a single system, around a center. This danger is only heightened by the circumstance that "English" is the imperial language. Yet there is no backing away . Consider, then, the direction Kamau Brathwaite takes when exploring the possibilities of Caribbean poetry: "Nation language is the language that is influenced very strongly by the African model, the African aspect of our New World/Caribbean heritage. English it may be in terms of its lexicon, but it is not English in terms of its syntax. And English it certainly is not in terms of its rhythm and timbre, its own sound explosions. In its contours, it is not English, even though the words, as you hear them, would be English to a greater or lesser degree." ("History of the Voice")

Thus the work remains a question of defamiliarizing language as a natural condition, of allowing poetry, a language within a language, to open like a sluice, of changing the language from the inside, of being aware of the silence within words that allows for such liberating motion, of arriving at a new language by way of an exploration of the old. That is to say, American is a post-colonial language too.

Individual consciousness liberates itself from the colonies English establishes within it by burning a new language within those very social cities so established by history. If the idea of the transcendental, which implies a detachment from the immediacy of the social, and the idea of the lyric, which implies an ecstatic upswell, still speak to us, it is because they allow us not a greater social mobility (obviously not!) but a mobility in the preconditions which make what is to follow possible — some kind of society.

Let us resolve to think of transcendental mobility — as a mobile. The poem as a mobile of words and signs, dangled over the crib of the culture, as to stimulate the mind to imagine new combinations. Patriarchal poetry? Perhaps. Matriarchal intentionality? No doubt. Childhood, that deep alembic, crawls to maturity in floods of light. Names of fruit nourish unusual bits of unconscious truth. *Attabi* was a neighborhood in Baghdad where a certain kind of patterned tapestry was made. The word that named that neighborhood traveled to English as "tabby," which became a kind of cat that bore a similar pattern in its fur. A tabby has wandered into the room just now. It is the ghost of my former pet. It stares at me blankly, its black nose still black, its expression as empty as when it was alive. That gaze is without meaning until I begin to write. Quite suddenly a real being is gazing back, not a ghost, not a cat either, but a being that overflows its name. Not Jabés, not Celan, not Weil, not Darwish. Not Dante or Ibn 'Arabi. But not uninformed by those names either. Amid the bounty of mid-summer a pair of eyes fill with signature and lament: broken, silent, resolute, voiced. At the fading ruins, they anticipate suns. Sediment is splendid. The dead and our living gaze are locked in love — and make for a third. The words are never just our own.

—L.S.

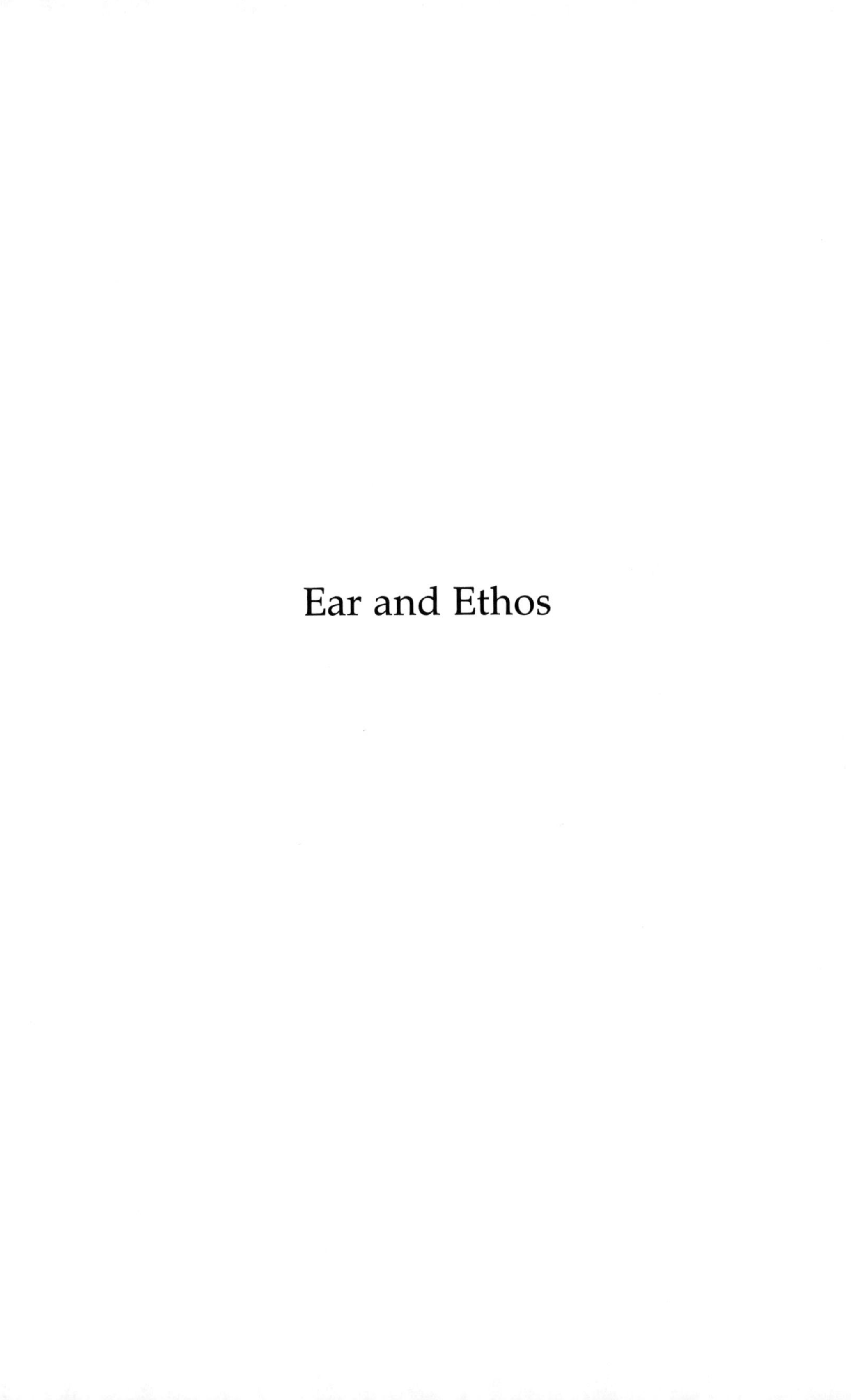

Ear and Ethos

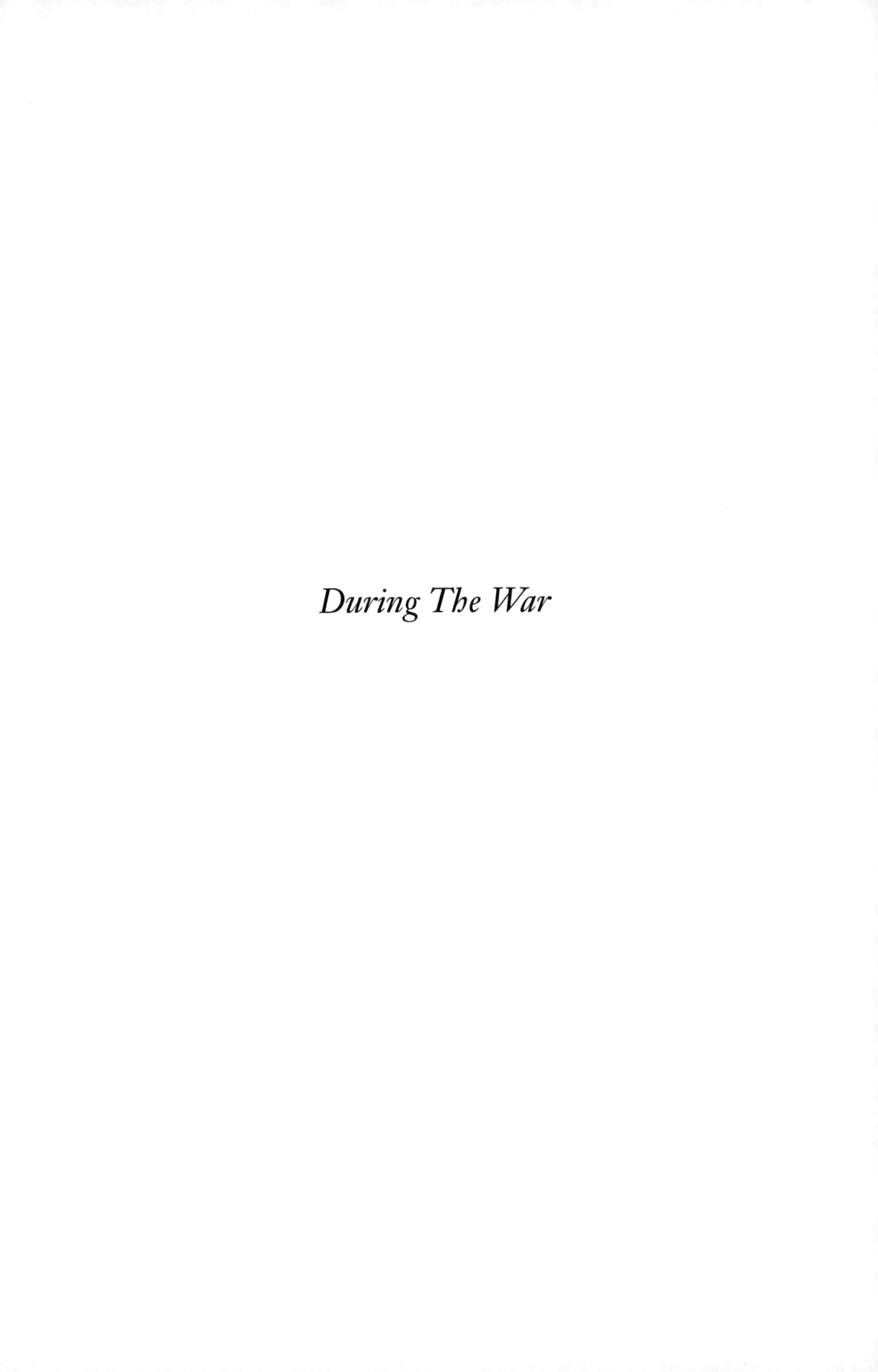

During The War

After Rumi

Don't go anywhere without me.
Say that sort of thing to squirrels
but they'll still scamper up trees,
not down your tresses,
it's just the way they are.
Or in the grass, in this world or that
location under the grass, you can say
"don't go" there. Better say
nothing. Language
says nothing about it.
Squirrel, I never spoke.

Don't go anywhere without me.
You can say it to your mallet while you work
but your mallet keeps on swinging
once you've gone to sleep,
your tongue keeps moving
once you think you're through conversing.
Words go all kinds of places
and leave me home only when they want to.

Nothing worse than to walk out along the street
don't go anywhere without me.
Don't get onto airplanes, don't go out to restaurants,
don't enter the apartments of women,
don't go there without me.

More than maps, more than love
don't go anywhere without me.
In case of nuclear attack

don't go anywhere without me.
Our world is coming to an end:
don't go anywhere without me.
Don't go anywhere without me.
Words go all kinds of places
and leave me home only when they want to.
Don't go anywhere without me.

Snow Flake In Sun Beam

A word that unchains from its prior definition is a lock that suddenly clicks.

"Tomorrow," a word so neatly bound. That it shows up today must be acknowledged, part of a potentially rich phrase that will yet tickle a horizon into form.

To spark, to flower, to think the next shift in a word, a meaning which neither of us will ever throat.

A poem pens its own openings, but locks itself up fast.

Impossibility of conjuring up that syntax that forms the yolk of speech:
to write as if from one's own exoskeleton.

Not a ditch in the mind, but a ditch in the ur-desert from which our minds spring.

Holding a poem to ones mind only confirms the original process.

Which could be a clue to the combination.

Bony sill of sorrow, dust in shaft of sunlight: snowflake, snowflake.

Only lucid if a star throws off sparks still rich with their own source:
O consort, will you join me to the horizon?

Like a fruit in full ripeness completely focused on itself.

That is torn, turned to nothingness, enters the landscape as writing.

Epilogue

A wind that kindles uncanny skin, freshets of feeling everyone in the village grows intoxicated in.

Desert poplars lost in swaying prayer and hummingbirds cups almost overflowing, bending to the wind.

A balm offered at no cost, the wind a nurse, the uncanny splendor of the invisible a living force ushered by the wind.

A man turns in the wind and glimpses his birth apart from any other birth. A woman turns in the wind and glimpses her birth, and then the birth of a twin. Triplets, quadruplets and quintuplets are born from the same womb in spectacular successive bursts.

A cooling wind no one in this hot village could even live without. Oh, its come before. An inner song a community whistles, sluice ways and ornate doors respectively rippling and whistling in its weird. Five of six sextuplets survey the cloudless sky, drinking wind.

All this and more the Air Force drops its bombs on, under jurisdiction of No Court, and at no cost to those who can neither imagine the wind or the bomb they paid to drop, leaving behind so much collateral damage.

Uncanny skin. Wind that stokes the flame in a patch of flaming desert. Weird wind. The waste wind blows. Windy, windy, windy mad.

Method

I walk past
and the tangerine unpeels:

I blink and electric-blue waves
inundate the A train. As for

domestic laughter, I've had to
give it up. This inexplicable brain,

all starfish and scissors, a cactus
that disobeys the laws

of its own ecology,
gets tangled in its own tissue.

Yet all night long I experience a radiance,
my retort to it flirtatious and cheeky.

I'm an inventor, quietly mapping
albino doors and pigmented windows;

obliged to beam I best flicker out.
I once saw a *bream* get a heart transplant;

they put inside him the heat of a star.
Though it is true all those lovely green octopi

pleasuring themselves in the penthouse
eventually were flung from the roof,

the crows grabbing 'em the moment
they hit the sidewalk. Or the Eurasian jackdaws.

Loosening the falcon of your dreams
till it soars as twelve tone music,

balling up all your mistakes
in a new fangled system, what's the difference:

outside of our imaginations
mangos juice us the most.

(I want to eat every mango
there ever was like a small

unemployed carpenter
not Christ, just a small, unemployed carpenter.)

A live hen feels sweaty
but it is for that feel that Ham's bazaar is thronged.

Each bird is pinched, then passed over,
to be pinched all over again several hands later.

Thoughtful lava bubbles over the boughs,
imprisoning the tall, lean trunk;

a lava wonderland, actually your own
magnetic passions, red as hemoglobin.

And just as a persimmons drops into an oasis pool
a little caravan of camels comes marching into view

like ants, like ants or like caramels
stuck at the bottom of a dry well.

Board me up. I no longer have the instinct
to officiate over my mental life.

For no emotion is ever local.

Insomnia

Worry that I'm not down for the night, out like a light, nocturnal sibling of that unspoken worry not to go down to Styx.

Does a clock worry hand to hand with its own ticking?

Writing is only the writing of insomnia, coaxing consciousness from brain — against the brain's grain.

Forlorn before the barrier of sleep what hurts about dying is that it hits with so many fists.

Insomnia, as such, is death's failure to control, its fury at not forming a perfect union with its victim, the fact of living in fits and starts, grappling with fiery wits.

A mind drowns in its pillow. But if it could swim under willows, in that joyous, shady brook you enter when only your unconscious drowns, then "Lethe" itself would provide the needed forty winks.

Styx is cognizant that it rubs down organisms, not cognizant that it would not flow without those organisms: reactive essence of hate.

In which you vie for your part, like a fire fly flickering in the spreading conflagration of biography.

Could passivity bypass passivity? A pass without gate? You do not fail from all words, only some.

The narrative says not to think for it.

Joycean Idyll

Syrupy tram
departing the tree, frozen to
the tree;
a frozen trouser sea,
core forming,
correspondence theory,
corporate;

dice
flung from a craggy hill,
fight elder after fight elder,
on the basis of box cars,
coining new
penis breaking
wars:

men proposing
to their mothers in dreams:
men piling up deer meat
in the back of pick up trucks:
all of them actually aging sons
gone to the Fair
for sheep shearing,
and Roth of the blurred hands,
and losing track of their own hands
near their knives and forks.

By schooner light and late night dory fin
we rue not bending to the water's face
sooner, much sooner, sooner, much sooner

before the war
while still the sap was running.

War Poem

What of old Mrs. Shea sprouting a beard, arguing with herself in the kitchen?

Oh, don't be alarmed, she's always that way, been daft for years and years, can't even hear her own voice.

Am I at home or in exile? All of us living in Baghdad now. (Stop this war with your ear.)

Certain villagers deep in the Vaucluse believe that a snake skin placed on the stomach will cure what ails you. I wouldn't know, I'm from Amityville.

Germaine halted in front of the birdbath. Its basin was half-filled with the unnamable.

The mind should be kept independent from the thoughts that arise within it.

Impossible. Sleep impossible. No more than the next thought is possible.

When my thoughts experienced a precision strike, images fell out of them at random.

A mobile kitchen had been set up not too far from there. The site was chosen at random. Whichever lucky refugees managed to make it out found the kitchen, seemingly god sent.

A cormorant stood on a piece of reef far out in the Dry Tortugas. One was black, one was red, one was a darker red.

Words continue to arrive from monitors stationed at highly equipped tracking stations. The networks are excited, they are people, they enjoy attention. Generals speak in abstractions when obliged to speak, real philosophers in thoughts. The pots and pans bubble with poison. Do you hear them bubbling?

In big cities and little cities big people and little people pretend not to pause from their work. They pause from their work. (Stop this war with your ear.)

No sooner had the pleasure given me by certain books aroused the demon of wishing to write then another demon rose and swallowed up the first. There was simply nothing to say.

My body tumbles into the ditch of language I've been forced to dig.

Let us not mince words, the letter the birds delivered was supposed to be a reminder of origin, a promise of salvation.

The act of simple naming the whole message itself.

The ringing of the other phone.

Primers of sound deposited in the marshy soil rise to the surface.

What of old Mrs. Shea sprouting a beard, cackling in the kitchen? Don't be alarmed, she's always that way, been daft for years and years, can't even hear her own voice.

The Eden Exhibit

1

The Eden Exhibit had already left town. But because I live here and have received instruction I recognized in your enthusiasm, striving towards the world, some trace of the unfettered energy one might have seen displayed there, hung in effigy.

2

Alive in a city of varied cuisines, on familiar terms with both its subways and its goats. You stare into the fisherman's bucket, nothing caught; copters hover low in search of god knows which suspect. Military in the streets, passing us as though they were already smoke and not sons and daughters, as if we had all gone up in smoke with them, all us voices gusting like ghosts between the power lines.

3

The city certainly has changed. Of course at each moment it was I who defined the limits of what I knew. Symbols contain emotional force but they are as much worm food as are these hands. All depths stream darkly muffled utterance. Then your voice calls me back to the immediacy of the alphabet, to a music rising ever again from the moment I had so fecklessly abandoned. What did you just say?

4

More and more free, like kites torn loose, each passing dog eliciting a cry of excitement. It is true that with love there are no strings attached. Breezes offer each other a secret sign.

5

Up a belated ladder, beginning to wonder is that a lake or a fog, an A or a D streaking up the tunnel? I've always felt anxious in supermarkets but you don't seem to notice; the whole lives only in its individual moments. And the physical separation between urban living and the land itself is supposed to be transcended by the presence of the park, these very grounds we now traverse, moving west to east, from golden horses to real ones of various adornment and color. Things sayable only to one who perceives things as such, in consonance with a source also mine.

6

Sometimes I must seem hard to you, the stars gathering and glittering in your eyes bursting with focus. Wash your hands, eat your noodles, pick up the clip, and so on. And all the while the bomb continues its downtown countdown. One, two, three, four, five, all gone. What is the name again of the city we live in? Our single shipwreck, the vanishing floor — a billiard ball tumbling from a newspaper and landing in the exploded room below.

7

The victors are served wine preserved in the mouth of a dead mother, signification itself the moment of violation. Each year makes up a new explanation. Each of us missing a chunk of name, or of brain, fences looped along the borders of identity, your toothless compatriots crying and crying and crying.

8

A man brings a bicycle aboard the A train. You point it out. I concede that a bicycle on a subway car is incongruous, though I've seen it many times before: the shiny metal, the motionless spokes, the silenced horn. This will be a short ride. W e are going our separate ways.

9

That afternoon, months before, walking along 16th Street, when I was overcome by the imprecise news of precision bombing, the proudly announced intention to decapitate, and cried live tears. How was I going to tell you about this, you who are already a veteran of these wars without even being conscious of them, you who are aware of each passing horse in the heart of the metropolis, so deeply in tune with the agrarian in the urban, the Rhinegold at the bottom of the Rhine?

10

Remember that time police cars converged, sirens blaring? I said, Forget the bus, lets grab a cab and get out of here. Lets get kicked out of a bar together, when they change the rules and don't permit kids to listen to the crooner. Lets scoff at the two year olds being wheeled in carriages, those glazed expressions pasted up and down their faces.

11

I'm talking about something like that, that day they began the bombing. But you know, I'm also here with you. Not even the slightest shadow encroaches upon this noon of encounter. Each corner articulate with particular impression, each musician that takes to the street that street's anima chivvied into expression. Every event is beyond prediction.

12

The nail of an idea goes into the plank of stupidity. But there is no guarantee that what will be built will not also be stupid. Just look around you. Y   ou do, and announce you want to build buildings, in spite of the power drills whose scream you scurry from. Conversant with poets and singers and doctors too you select " to build buildings," and also, " to farm cheetahs." To raise cheetahs, right? Yes, that's right, to farm cheetahs, to farm panthers, to farm panthers and cheetahs. Fine, I will support you in those endeavors. We haven't been to the galleries lately. Lets run for it.

John Brown's Body

There is so little that is individual and just.
You would think we had never been bees and beekeepers
collaborating on honey. In the hive of the subway
we glimpse guitar players singing sadly in Spanish.
Together on the couch the daughter laughs
and, outfitted in maiden speech, playfully
speaks the line: "read 'to be or not to be'
not the right way."At her father's behest she will squirt
the curvaceous woman in the playground who isn't yet
wet enough. Already she mouths the word "moldering,"
munches banana chips on the 2 train, meditates on colors.
The first guitar and the one not yet strung
tune themselves together, preparing a next song.
Like chinchillas, nipping mischieviously
at fingers extended through the cage, highly American.
As in provoke something. Fight for the familiar things
the patriots only pretend to stand for. In Thoreau's words
let your life be a counter-friction to stop the machine.
There is so little that is individual and just.

What Other

Six Ways Two Places At Once

1

Collage is empty
and the gorge of the frogs

mighty deep,

everyone in that valley,
including the frogs,

as silent as yucca.

Tacit tanks target distant ocean's waves
human rights receding, crash of armored tide
now bobs, now bombs
news of the heavy wedding many dead
and child's brightly naked teeth.

And the wind in the oak leaves
as soundproofed
as the inside of a lobster.

The cueing machine tells of spring snow.
The cueing machine tells of spring snow
but I once rode an escalator which,
without warning, reversed directions.

The Pentagon rises like a phoenix,
even larger than before.

Groaning under an Administration
steeped in oil, lighting fires as it steeps.

"To keep the whole capacity
of the potential intellect
constantly actualized."
To keep the whole capacity
of the potential intellect
constantly actualized

and now, if your ears are nimble,
you can hear July 4th frogs
proposing to July 4th frogs
in the gully of July 5th.

2

The silence of perception
is the flesh of the book
opening itself
to the wondering reader.

And the name aids you
in its very impenetrability.
Nature fills the emptiness of the sign.

Music/mother tongue
a clarinet shines
like a sealskin.

Listen:
the life-world of the destroyer-nation
surly with commuter traffic,
its deepest consonances
muffled.

Look: a TV nailed to an oak tree
transfixes the worshippers in deafening.

Listen, look:
the polymorphously conceptual Father
a harbor seal barking philosophy from the piers
and the rocks.
Proteus is his name.
Proteus is also rich, dark coffee.

Have skimmed for a word of the first language
in a black bound Bible
and in the dismantled lightening
lining the heavily trafficked
super highways.

Road kill after road kill,
Proteus-bled.

The silence of perception
is the cry inside the flesh
surging towards
the letters of its exile.

3

Memory passes into formal knowledge; knowledge begets
capacity and power; power permits forgetfulness.

Such is the symmetry of the two-way bridge
between oppressor and oppressed.

Amongst all the atrocities
 I shrug,
motoring in my new car
up the causeway, out past
Indulgence Farm — that robust enterprise —
far from the light of the little lighthouse
of First Anger.

Nix to logic,
nein to recognition,
nope to news
that stays news.

Nay too to the opposable human thumb?

Blood off the coastal waters:
the radio says you are better off

taking the bridge.

To wipe the footprints of toppled towers
off of curtainless cities
through whose windows
the moon stares:

to wipe the fingerprints off murdered continents.

Thus the Jenin atrocities were never documented.

I'll take the bridge

I'm taking the bridge right now

not to plunge into the morass
the private drama of guilt

is merely the scum over,
not the climax.

4

Taught to fear
    complexity, —
to beware shifting
    boundaries,
the self insists on boundaries
hard and fast.
Or so the moral community
    proposes,
its posture headquartered in pious depression about
its own fate, its lack of reputation
    in consumer society,
and most of all, its absence *of courage*.

Never assume there is one
    who can speak clearly
into the contradictions
of non-identity and loss
or that such a person's
knowledge of suffering
extends to his organization, or to us.

Yet there *is* a victim under all the formulas,
surreptitiously subscribed to and conceded
by all to be a *necessary evil*,
denied any intellectual
status or *recognition* by all parties involved
because less valued.

What's worse,
men who out
of the desperation of their lives
try not to exist
by blowing up the dancers
with themselves?
Or a whole system
howling "Sub-Humans"
and acting on that precept,
having pursued in tanks
    the tortured
right into their ruined hives?

I grow strong hearing myself
unable to justify it all,
falling silent . . .
false words only promote
the affliction.

Security forces preempt security
in favor of their own
regularly scheduled
programming.

5

Occupation again, and the tanks that bring occupation
arrive to padlock every dimension of everyone's life.

After the military incursions
ethical fires burn in every woodland
of A country, in every city where the incursion is applauded,
    urged, rationalized,

in every room where persons not in that room
have *their* existence denied.

1) After the burnt offerings and the black milk...
2) After the bulldozers and the bantustans
3) Tears pour forth from nubile ground.
4) And the stars, full throated and welling.
5) A peacock broadcasts theology.
6) Violence will not be put to rest by violence.
7) Only after acts of creation can come a day of rest.
7) Violence will not be put to rest by violence.
7) There is no Sabbath during occupation.

7) And Occupation said
let there be light:

A leprous light entrenches itself during occupation.
No ambassador from these fingers to those,
not in this leprosy.
Theology infiltrates the very stones;
7) geology is theology is fence.

7) Marina Tsvateyva once wrote
"All poets are Palestinians."
While an Israeli who writes in Arabic —
an Arab Jew, he longs for Baghdad
before the expulsion — unfurls his latest text.

7) Helicopters empty their fire, tanks roll, writers write,
as Jenin takes place, echoing Shatila.
From the Negev to New York
my tribe is going mad.
In my distress I call upon a Lord
I don't believe in (7)
but the Jewish Arab

from Baghdad, writing in a language
his new land despises
dreams for seven nights
 is *real* . . .

The very being of language
implies an other with whom to speak.
Language is always the other spoken to.
Each hill of Jerusalem knows that,
next year in
cry indeed unto.
next year in.

6

My city once achieved fame
for its disclosure
of an unknown language
within a language

that yet remained mysterious.

Now sacred and profane wars
flush out all vanity
from the tall grass
of former meadows and woodlands.

Day and night an outpouring
of scare tactic warnings
trade on the gap between
words and awareness,

zones of ambiguous utterance
closed by the authorities
until further announcement.
Liberty Avenue and
the slave burial ground
form a single Main Street.

The new militarism annexes my sleep.
Sacred and profane conspire to justify
the one disconnect.
Sacred and profane
justify garrisons
in rainforests
and peach orchards.
The city beckons me into its logic
of mutually assured midnights.
Each siren announcing the last siren.
Each emergency an ember of all emergency.

Not that fire but another fire.
Not bomb by bomb obliterating
more merchandise
Empire then remaps
in its own image,
but instead witnessing
an image you'd never have guessed at
emerge from emergency.

Born of a love with no past
a city speaks within us
in unexpected journeys,
wine-dark dictionaries
foaming with words and opacities.

"Birthday of a new world"
Thomas Paine wrote in his proposal
for American revolution:

black copters crouched
in newfangled flowers.

Invitation

>   —*Rodrigo Toscano*

No symphony proves fruitful,
>   or Hebron.
Not theoretical considerations, not physical existence,
>   or Hebron.
To say "information" is not information
but an inkling of intensive form.
But do we, literally, unfathomable?
>   Say "Jenin," say "Nablus."
This will not be true of an inessential content
or Gaza.
And for each crutch sat seven without limbs.
>   Or Tulkarm, or Ramallah.
In a mode
forgotten to man,
a million inmates.
Or Gaza.

All our tumult
tumbles into words,
turning them to windows of salt.
Of cells and sun
falling on the prison cells,
the sharpest rays illuminate
the longest jail blocks,
they will grow in the sunlight

of a special economy.
An original, profoundly superficial,
                or Jenin.
Scores of dead, send in
live doves. Each hoe held in the hand
of a hated rival. Beat their beaks.
Not grasp the birth pangs of a twig.
Say information, say to a woman
"Gaza, strip."
Occupied by one's own gaze,
seeing only what one wants to see.
          Or Bethlehem.

Yes.
Yes, your visa will expire at the end of this poem.
Yes, you will need a new passport to exit
this nightmare, a new genre of passport.
If every veteran of reality rose up and protested
every single case of war mongering
                or Jenin.
In the prison yard convenes a court
for shooting hoops. Shooting hopes,
all who enter here.
                Or Hebron.
Unlike the words of the original text
orthodox experiences remains fire-proof:
just give me the rock.
Pass me the damn Dome of the Rock
or rebound it, rebind it, ban travel both ways,
          or Bethlehem.
Dribbled away in a mode
forgotten to free men,
which the Committee against Torture
finds to constitute torture.
Never to liberate the language
imprisoned in the rock.

The Tomb of the Patriarchs, forever and ever.
Oh, he was wed to his wines, cheap as chickens.
And of course he was strung out,
which is his God Given Right.
                Or Qalqiliya.
Slapped buttocks
in explicit jeans
no one dares talk about.
                Or Tulkarm.
Didn't the river need seven dams to block its waves?
A freshly pierced goat's heart,
flung into the tracks tank treads leave
in mingled bloods and mud.
These lands of little men.
In their white frothy bliss,
their ability not to see,
steak for me and steel for you,
doctors without borders for all those devils
inconveniently jostled,
kept by curfew from even their cemeteries.
But the cemetery is our library,
our archive, our garden!
This is not true of an inessential content,
or Gaza.
This is forever, for forever and ever.
                Or Nablus.

This is forever, for forever and ever.
Trauma irrigates new channels of hate.
                Or "Hebron":
a decisive detail evolving only in language,
a flux substantiating the published,
or Gaza.
                Beit Rama, Salfit, Artas,

a liquid spectacle of "facts on the ground,"
forced to strip and march at gunpoint.
                    Or Ramallah.
Unable to grow a single blade of grass
without the Others permission.
Did I mention the moon
reflected in the silent waters
of the Dead Sea?
That you thought you had done with crossing
sad tracts of land, those that made of you and your travails
amazing additions to the constant stone you wearied?
                    Or Jericho.

Dearest Father
(important listener)
ask that ancient washerwoman
if there is anything left to wash,
anything left to grow.
                    Or Ramallah.
Dearest Rumi says that if you are unthankful for the fruit
all the other forms turn ugly too.
                    Or Hebron.
The belt that is the waist about to heal.
Dearest olive groves confiscated by the courts.
The waist that will not heal, freshly belted.
Never felt living beings within you?
Visit this cemetery,
dig into these roots of light,
lose yourself in earth.
Silence capsizes into a glass kingdom,
vast and perceptual, shattering
all your links to the former caravan.

Dearest Mother.
                    Or Hebron.

Sand the color of shattered stone,
in which sits a big part of my past.
Dearest Mother,
calling Gaza.
Dearest Mother, dearest Father.
Land that sobs from its own contractions,
never rid of itself, syntax beyond aching,
never actually giving birth.
Quivering in the wheatfield
from so much female,
too many mounds of remembrance,
too much musk and haunch.
And the sun clasps all of it,
blood-stained and precious,
to its sensors.
Calling Gaza.
Culling Gaza.
Calling Gaza.
       Or Hebron.
To say "information" is not information
but an inkling of intensive form.
Of necessity therefore the demand
for literalness.
Gaza.
       Or Hebron.

Occupational Hazards

Palestinian Transfer

Of olive groves spread out across soft hills the people despair: *everything here has been marked, and everything marked is lost.*

Transfer isn't necessarily a dramatic event.

The telephone just keeps ringing and ringing. Something like a stethoscope against the breast. Clinical.

In this way three children break an afternoon curfew and are mortally wounded.

The current situation calls for a swift and speedy effort to control all forces: not only as freedom struggling with its conqueror, refusing its reification and its perverted image, but as the being of groves spread across the hills, raising their fruits like tiny fists, by some unimaginable patience holding back the punch that would provoke the conqueror further.

The ruined, arid land, the neglected trees, testify that promises nourished from afar didn't create an organism strong enough to withstand the assorted — well, you know all that already. Like a stethoscope against the chest.

To show how and why a non-violent person, like myself, becomes violent. Not that I have become violent.

Uneasy rapprochement, for the sake of others. That explains the contradictory character certain states of mind are charged with, a clap of thunder when no storm is visible.

As for the psycho-social trance I would like to say one last thing about Steven Biko.

Festering wounds ask questions of their father. Like a refrigerator that groans from its own inner cold. The telephone just keeps ringing and ringing.

The 36

It was while the army demolished a neighboring house, belonging to the family of a militant from Islamic Jihad, that the wall fell on the Makadmah family.

Opposition came swiftly from the 36 hidden justices.

There they are, you will have to go a long way around if you want to avoid them.

I would like to stroll within range of your rifle. I'm that angry.

Then an explosion, and the wall fell on the assembled family.

The name might be derived from a root meaning "to come" or "be present": or possibly from another one meaning "to bruise."

The last child the father and his neighbors found, scratched but alive.

Beauty is enhanced by this single moment of peace, and his hand, which clutches the rubber ball, and Being never at any time running its course with cause and effect coherence.

That our predicates do not contain untruths but are simply claims gone unfulfilled in our contemporaries and in us. Being-in-the-thick-of-it.

When the building came down I felt a disconnect, a complete loss of apperception, as well as a completely leveled perception of things.

Mountains of night creep away without ever again yielding to barest day.

With ambulances blocked from reaching the scene, Mrs. Makadmah, 41, died while neighbors were carrying her to a clinic.

Her name might be derived from a root meaning "to come" or "be present," or possibly from another one meaning, "to bruise."

Expect no trial.

Except in every single action we are engaged in.

Possibly mixed among our neighbors, the 36, hidden and just.

Concentrated within themselves they go unrecognized by their fellow men.

Mrs. Makadmah was known as an excellent cook who often made cakes and cookies for her children.

The Israeli Army expressed regret.

Click Here to Receive 50% Off Home Delivery of The New York Times.

Essential Services

Essential services in several critical areas, including health, education, water, electricity and law enforcement could no longer be provided.

What good would running to the Occupied Territories have done, what good running away ?

The bridge, much like the airport, the border crossing or any other entry point, is a place of enduring humiliations — homologue to the denial of history.

The fiancée arrived, surrounded by her brothers and sisters, all seven of them.

This quarter 17 killings were carried out that were almost certainly assassinations.

My grandmother and grandfather go to the rail of the boardwalk and look down at the beach.

If you throw even a cursory glance at the past you will observe that in the continuum of colonial control apartheid and peace have never been coextensive.

After his village was razed the Leper approached the soldier cradling his Uzi.

The ocean is becoming rough; my grandmother observes that the waves come slowly, drawing their strength from far back.

With pious and gentle resignation the persecuted ones suffered such intolerance (though later, in the Warsaw Ghetto . . .)

If the Law is texture, that texture must have changed. Been smoothed out by its "triumphs."

To cope with interruptions and delays all schools in the West Bank begin to make up classes, when possible, during off days and holidays, as if by the sheer quantity of hours the circumstance could be overwhelmed.

The power of redemption seems to be built into the clockwork of life.

Out of stasis and paralysis, symptomatic of ghettos in general, I decided to run there and not to run there.

A stone   roars   like   a   bird   Slaughtered
Tahseen Alkhateeb writes from Amman.

Not genocide, not ethnic cleansing: a name has yet to be conceived for what is undergone in these curfewed quarters.

Certainly not "The Question of Settlements."

The Argentines speak of "the annihilated" but that isn't it either.

Redemption and its blasted clockwork.

Penelope

She set up a great loom in the main hall, started to weave a fabric with a very fine thread. And every night, when the wooers had fallen asleep, she would unthread that day's work.

Penelope transfers her strength to the medium of her subjective expression, in order to then subordinate herself to that medium, more than subjective, in the act of destructive defiance.

On the other side: only eight outposts established since 1996 have been completely dismantled. Many see this expansion as positive.

Weaving done in oneself insures that one won't spill a drop of another. Then one undoes one's own weaving. This is not just a ruse.

The awesome power of sacrifice. I tracked its meaning, never examining the sources of power that allowed me to make my own tracks, and thus, erasing them in the process.

Every day I would weave my father-in-law's shroud, and every night by torchlight I would unweave that same web.

At least let her finish her weaving before you possess her. No. The bulldozer kept coming.

I'm no expert but I think I see a problem here.

If Palestine is Penelope, Penelope has already waited more than 54 years.

Preoccupation

The first haiku's task is to achieve exemption from someone in purdah walking on your
street.

The second haiku's task is to achieve exemption from someone in a tallis walking on your
street.

The real haiku has no task.

Redemption and its blasted clockwork.

Odysseus

Other tales there are to tell, almost as sad, said Odysseus.

Words gather inside those exiled from space, those receding into time. Treat the person in whom they gather as if that person were their own sick child. Like parents made magically young in the tending.

You seek a homecoming as sweet as honey, since once every soul and soul-root had its special place in the pleroma. All instantiations of the return prove false. All fixed images of home prove idol.

Yet contagious as laughter or yawning there remains an unfathomable quality that frees language from something like description. Which remains undescribed, tantalizing.

Every day I would weave at the great loom; every night I would tear my work to shreds.

My guiding light, said Penelope, is the Israelites: they waited two millennia.

Under the name Reb Areb the poet Jabès offers: "Jewish solidarity is the impossible passion one stranger can feel for another."

Penelope, calm and straightforward: "death will surely come to the suitors."

He stripped off his rags and revealed himself as who he really was: a seed in the celestial granary, the perfect tension between particularism and universality, the voluptuous pleasure of silence fusing with anger.

Penelope one's waiting, Odysseus one's wandering.

Odysseus always no more than Penelope at her loom, weaving the future.

He her thought now, she thinks, in one guise or another   , for more than two millennia.

Elixir of Listening

The Steam Bath

Steam billows into the steam room,
and frozen minds in their showcases
melt to the ground, wet and round,
like little children with God's eyes
flowering enormous feelings.

Bathing in some kind of inner source
pouring out, heating up, pouring out,
adjusting to the forms dipped into it:
steam outmaneuvers the strongman,
steam evaporates everything
but the buckle on the belt of power,
steam moistens every clay cup
suddenly perspiring milk and beer
from inside its own thirst.

Offer up this cup of silence; it figures
that this voice of all voices should call through steam.

This voice *is* steam, and lust spattered loins
look holy.

Here the wind and the leaf forget the necessity
for the leaf to part.

A village is a single embrace,
a waiter and waitress closing a café.
Forest creatures drink from the dish rack.

A firm buttocks provides the finest pillow.

Then the steam turns to sermon.

Figures sink back into bags of wind, eyes buttered,
ears like bribes.
Being freezes over, outside and in.
Breathing fills with drains.

We stand in the sheepfold of this skin and turn unconscious.

Yet no one can prove a momentary expansion didn't happen.
Even as each of us sinks his chin into deeper and deeper forms of poverty
it is true that later more steam can always be ladled.

The Stream

The stream needs me to be here to run through this meadow and there is no humiliation in being a patch of ground, nor is there dread in the heart of the angel upon realizing his wings are spread in a tar pit.

All these leaves setting up shop on my easel are entirely a matter of my own expectation. Yes, but if you canoe by the right open window, a government will be seen giving itself to someone else, which would explain why this year summer is leaving us out.

Think of it as too much heat, so much sunburn saved. I would have been naked, right? Haven't I always been kind of frowning with flame, like all those woods evidently still wintering, still hesitant about getting into the foliage?

OK, I concede that love never outgrows the forest of the maternal, those thickets in which the dunce of language loses himself.

OK, oranges are gleaming sources.

Nothing will ever wrangle those oranges from the trees, groves and groves of them.

An almost muscular moon suddenly experiences an earthquake, ivory keyboards first picking up a vibration that squishes and rages and rats on us.

A ray of sunlight picks the moon right from the sky.

I'm just one raspberry falling into the cup.

Tree of Life

As chlorophyll drains from leaves
and their skin flames in brilliant tumbling colors,
just so productive being rises from our consumer selves.
Its not so much dying as it is writhing,
not so much Fall as it is frail,
crackling bodies the fuel for crackling bodies.
Only what one has made for oneself
is of any use in the extremity
of this passage's seduction,
these waves of light like tree's fervent dreams.
Gods do not make men; men make gods.
Only the daemonic valorization of production is productive.
The mind is clear on that. The skin of leaves is true.

Summer Vacation

Sand in the waves
makes the mind immense:

rain catches in the death jar.

It isn't because of the rain
that the doe falters.

And as the stupor clears
your mind still crests

remember to cry to the sun
remember to rise near the sun

without burning
your Icarus voice

no yellow base to the black strings
of the shiitake mind,

no golden base
to the vase.

Lets grill shrimp
right up against Helios's side,

piss in great joyous streams
against the side of his house.

You in your pinhole aviary,
I this side of the crystal storeroom

from which we derive our bones,
wrenched from the shiitake womb

to natural shocks,
the absolute as real as a poker chip.

The fox
encounters his food.

But the waves
refuse to gift.

The leash leaps.
But the epicenter is already crammed.

Al Fresco

To talk *al fresco*, to the beat of prior drums, of a past in common, and a ladder . To raise yourself up as your own mitt.

A ball thumps down into the now: this catch of words.

Which furnishes us with a common tongue: you only borrow from it to insist upon who is who, I to find out who I am. Both of us turn out to be wrong. That would be why you and I are drawn to these window sills, not to jump but to jabber, and then to glare redly across. daring that now , if I did. Please believe me when I say my intentions were good. I have a clear conscience, like seals, whales and other mammals that also dive.

Our mother tongue even strikes us as odd. Thus I am exceedingly familiar with a cot strewn with my own oddities. To which I add, "I will calmly sip my words out of a language that pools on the high plateau, drinking until the autumn freeze necessitates definition."

But had I not first said, "I did not rob your soul, I robbed a soul for you?" I apologize for Dust forms dust. What forms form? Some shared genetic material, a revolution or a standing still, a play of light and never-will-be-light, war wounds and wounds you cannot see, the living and the left behind. So dim now, I cannot tell them apart.

To hold hands with contradiction.

Cliff abyss open parenthesis

Apple Anyone

Apple Anyone 1

Shall I portray you as a blazing afternoon?
The freaking almanac didn't forecast amber rain.
Wind whipped to shreds ballyhooed Doppler readings
As your typhoon tongue lashed my latest wants.
So the sun's golden boasts are bested by bullying clouds,
each of our arsenals costing us our alchemy.
Yet no cloud shall dim my love's manic barbs.
Neither will my eyes become gauze, or ghouls;
no Nothingness shall brag of drowning me in Styx.
A single whiff from the carafe of years suggests there is more
to speech, a crocus thrusts at the barbarian of description.
As long as its a carob for a carob, a copt for a copt, bedouins
lead us far into an arch-alcohol we're the ones to ferment.

almanac typhoon arsenal alchemy gauze ghoul carafe crocus barbarian carob Copt Bedouin alcohol

Apple Anyone 2

You are more orange than oranges, more red than blood orange.
Coffee masks enervation, I'm still awake, checkmated by night;
life packs in too much racket to know calm's truest state and form.
And during the day its way too hot, thanks to the pushy sun.
Thus the safari is unshackled from its safety net.
So rice is checked, guitars jar, spinach is lacquered in a can.
In the constant flux of things all good from goods must fail.
But you do not mask from sight those gifts you possess,
alchemy on a wavy mattress among lightly waving fronds.
In words to you groves will always glow, the purpose
of so many night presences suddenly made lilac.
So long as poets pick fruit, these hands pick you.

orange   coffee   checkmate   safari   rice   guitar   jar   spinach   lacquer   mask
alchemy   mattress   lilac

Apple Anyone 3

As big waves flip out onto rocky coast so our days finish abruptly.
The ocean's tributaries show their dhows: appearance is a cipher.
As childhood, that deep alembic, in floods of light
crawls to maturity, where which to crouch, calling itself a King.
And as we change positions with what was finishing at our birth
hope builds its harem in serif, like rice collecting saffron.
A guitar-shaped bench trembles to its own rhythm!
Light wants to fix in place the flourish it dabs on things —
this great esplanade of sesame, magazines wide,
something wished for, made of marabout and lime.
As names of fruit nourish unusual bits of unconscious truth.
Nothing is born but for the sword to assassinate
and still, in their hiddenness, from red shift to red shift
I praise your alcoves, and the oceans wildest dilations.

dhow cipher alembic harem serif saffron guitar sesame magazine
marabout lime assassinate alcove

Apple Anyone 4

I'm not going to dignify the proposition
that this our hazardous union of minds

has flaws — a kiss is not a kiss
which scuffs if it finds some scuffing.

I'm talking about a tattoo in thought,
something that can't be erased by monsoon's anger.

When you garb yourself for love, think sequined sash,
damasked but garbled minaret:

Something that will appear a star for all those sailors
of unknown worth, like us, fleeing the latest massacre.

Constancy is no clock's fool; like kohl to lid
ear clings to lip until the drop-off point of doom.

If you can cinch it that I'm wrong, I'll shut up,
drop all my claims concerning the human carat.

hazard   tattoo   monsoon   garb   sash   damask   minaret   massacre   kohl   carat

Why is it my words always touch this particular?
I stay afloat on language I've plucked from Sufi summer,
my trysts with words the same one wooed, mascared, talced.
Though the lute of a genii is as outdated as last year's atlas,
though a belated troubadour sings of checkmate move by move,
yet no monumental rock shall outlast these our silly constructs:
that which glints brightly in such tariffed compositions
is a gazelle among orange groves, a mecca in the mouth.
Here comes a tabby whose scratch will leave a lasting mark,
or else a taffeta from a quarter of town recently hit by bombs,
or all the cotton ever picked, the laborious wizard enslaved inside you.
Why is it my words always touch this one particular?
As the sun is daily both bouncy and flat so we transact
only what we can minaret, darting among damasked ruins.

Sufi mascara talc genii atlas troubadour checkmate tariff gazelle orange
mecca tabby taffeta cotton wizard minaret damask

Apple Anyone 6

To go on in an ideology that is patrolled by admirals
all praised to the hilt, each awarded triple scoops of sherbet,
sugars gushing in banana and lime, or to grab up pails against
a whole Mediterranean of pain, and by opposing, drain it?
The road to Baghdad: it is an orgasm religiously sought.
To slow my brain and by night to say we stopped all that:
a saffroned vulture scuffs the dirt it lands in until every man
looks inward, acknowledging his own mulatto ground
and the thousand gauzy masks our bodies are mom to.
To slow my brain — to slow my brain!
And during that slowing to succumb to a new fantasy,
a woman with corneas like coffee beans, a coiled mortality
uncoiling, amalgam, not amalgam, that is not a jackal —
a vocabulary, a calamity, and at last, a casualty list.

admiral   sherbet   sugar   banana   lime   Baghdad   saffron   mulatto   gauze
cornea   coffee   amalgam

Apple Anyone 7

I lost contact with you for just one morning and all the music
turned to arsenic, in my mind I barely maintained your image.
Now, while you dream of ponies, petals gush from your eyes:
apricot o'clock, orange o'clock, after which comes lime.
So I am partly blind and partly sighted, like those blue shrubs
reputed to be filled with elixir of bird when all they really do
is interlock with whatever happens to pass, in pure contingency,
and its mostly birds, and grains of sugar, and amulet candy.
Over these shifting truths the mind has no hold, our hands
liming mascara into the tabbied skin of twilight, talismanic hour.
Mountain top and salt spray gush, all part of your massage.
Don't be naïve: they can send assassins by guitar too.
Yet quietude fills the carafe of hours, orange fills that quietude,
there is nothing yet to mourn: you are here, it is all still here.

guitar arsenic apricot orange lime shrub elixir sugar amulet candy
mascara tabby talisman gush massage

Zero Hour

Last night a bit of moon appeared above this candle.
Coffee fell hotly into cups, so many footsteps of walking dream.
I sensed certain life forms, normally shy, strain against
their ghoul-freaked masks, seek the burning candle.
Then there was only the burning candle, nothing sought.
A single column of smoke rising beautifully and in error
as if beyond all amber, a single throat swaying
like some delicate giraffe's aloft over massaged savannah.
Alcohol sparkled on the way from the carafe;
on the sequined sofa of night I distinctly tasted scallion.
I beheld a compass and the first apricot of our being,
the algebra of musk and a throne of smoke thrumming grievously
in an ancient alcove, beyond mortal argument.
"I" is anchorless but authentic.
"I" is wax wetting the crimson amulet its held in.
"I": a vocabulary, a calamity, a list of other voices.

crimson coffee ghoul amber giraffe massage savannah alcohol carafe
sequin sofa scallion apricot algebra alcove amulet

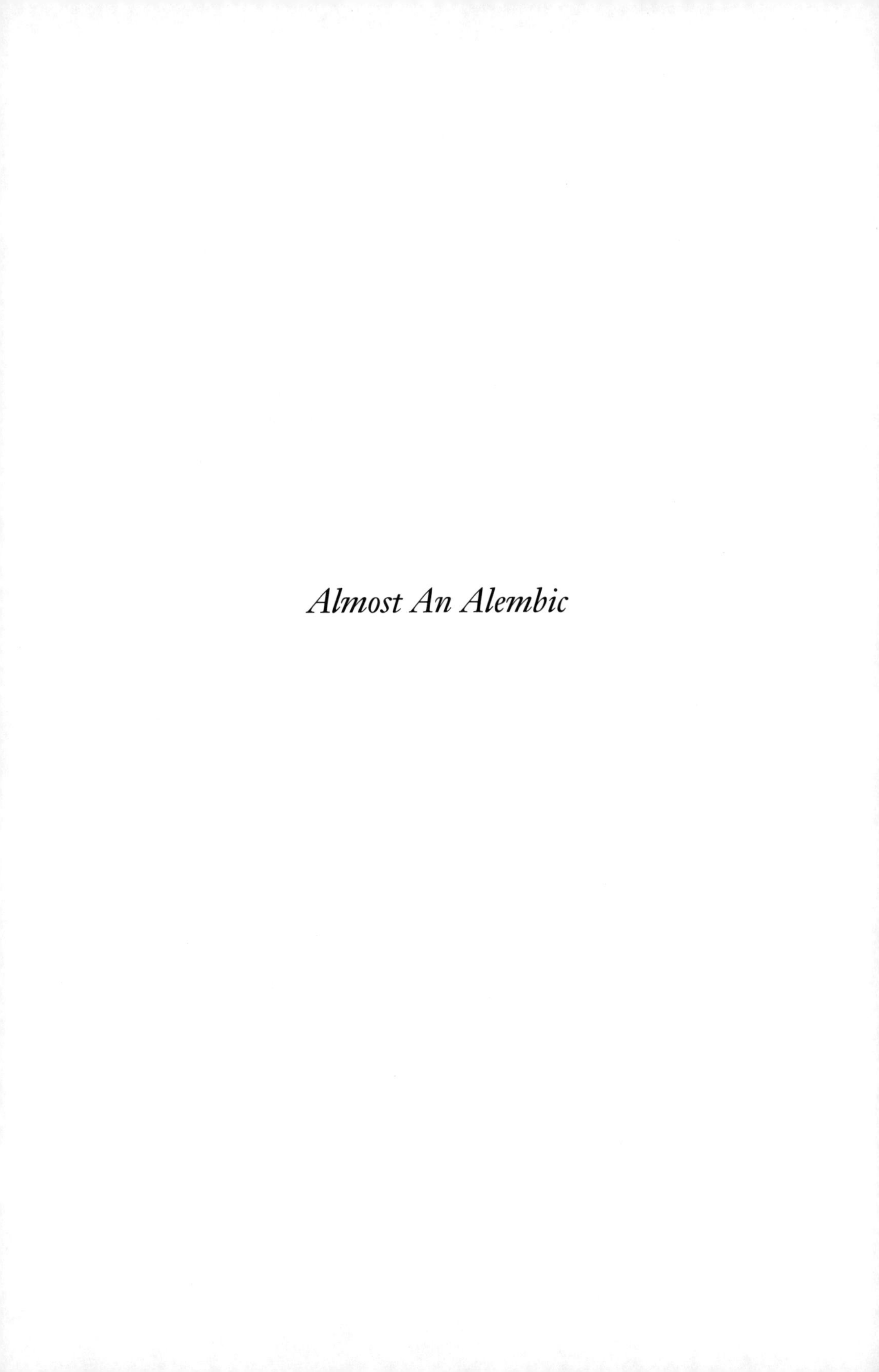

Almost An Alembic

Sheep's Head

An hour came
I could no longer
hide from.

At the hour
I needed Notung —

at the hour I needed to *believe*
a Jess collage was going to transform me —

for that magic instant that Klee creates
in almost his every image —

There was only
my own absence.

The words had failed.
Or I had failed the words.
It didn't matter.
Black fact of that which
    cannot be said
just the tip of a black, black
iceberg. It was the iceberg of a life
adrift on an oiled sea
but I won't go further into
what I've wasted.

My grandmother's painting of a heart, the one with
    a large black tear
spilling from its right ventricle,

something she'd painted
just before her heart attack

and then forgotten about till months
or was it years later —

stares at me, crawling with spiders
and signs.

One hundred Confucian scholars
couldn't help me think
clearly
about that gesticulating spider,
or this cul-de-sac of being
I've created.

Full breasts in the other painting —
that might help
but its only a painting.

Where is Notung when I need it —

Where is Klee's
"The Man with One Wing" —

Walking the rooms
I stare hard at Neptune's mask
hanging in the hallway.

After all Neptune lords it over the deep
as well as the hallway.
And it is only his depths
that can overwhelm the facts —

like so much flotsam and twig.

The Library of Seven Readings

I

Because its material substratum remains transcendental
the freedom of the subject, which the transcendental is designed to rejuvenate,
allows us to inhale and exhale refreshing drafts just as we approach the summit.

Because you're transcendental anger remains so materially touchy
the aether's freedom has been replaced, by common consent, by this frozen
partition, each side overcome at being singled out and laurelled.

So too the liberty of the subject, which this device is designed to rescue,
whose walls have all but disappeared via benign invasion,
diffuses back into a more personal embassy, where it can be better monitored.

As a good pianist will adjust the piano stool before he plays
so too the secular basis detaches itself from its ground
and declares that its own home is an independent realm in the clouds.

He nodded vigorously to communicate his delight at this news.
From one shore of the carbonated continent to the other,
the process of dividing property. I think it must have released
                              some secret anger in me

But its material substratum remained transcendental.
So too the freedom of the subject, which this device fails to rescue,
is fragile and always something else, a seashell awed at being singled out.

Therefore the individual as he appears in this world of prose
literally refers to the highest point in the heavens
and cuts you your first bits of meat, if you remember it.

To insist the image of the beloved remain manifest even as synthesis takes place.
To freeze into an idol a fruit orchard that flickers with the knowledge of likeness.
Or language true to the experience of language, eternity babbling at the edge

Of formal negation, a declaration of solidity that melts into air. As when
Anna Livia Plurabelle was driven from Schloss Paradise and fell under the Law
of the Tree of Porridge, life slow-as-molasses dripping from its drooping boughs.

The alternative translation for this passage, one I have tentatively adopted,
reads: "Whose mouth is the smallest of all springs yet quenches our material
desire by running through the holiest shrines (simplest magic discovered last)."

The fact is, the soul is moved about only by the violent poking of an angel
of different condition, then strives to become an actor freed from its lines,
finally struts away from all demands of Script and the Prison-house of Eden.

And yes, singly or in pairs, as if to apologize for still being present
where there was never any ground, tears appeared in my mother's eyes,
passionate constructions no two people could ever dream in tandem.

II

Thanks to the material substratum remaining just as you have seen above
I hear a voice that is mine, and then another voice, that is not.
Which relates to how we notice that clutching ice is a delight to the girl.

She was so enthusiastic that it was touching.
All appeared new, dazzling at first, inexpressibly strange and delightful.
And then suddenly, no new words appeared in my book, even the blank pages

Were veiled from view, deep down, far-off, invisible
a paucity of instruction drawn straight from a passive hell,
fear bouncing around and around the very walls that successfully buffalo us.

After a good pianist adjusts the piano stool, and warms his or her fingers,
what follows instead is a harmony between the Creator and the True God
as from a cocoon of thought about thought, and then, to become aware of death

Veiled from view, deep down, even invisible, but not far off.
In the absence of any systematic technique for overcoming suffering from within
the music tries to identify itself only with what the living cannot do without

In ever more varied combinations. From above the moon to beneath the squid
an increasing surplus of fancy gizmos substitutes for community and things,
everything that really happens, happening within a blind auditory world

Just as the poem at hand seeks to negate the immediate
by the abstraction of its particular choice of a beloved.
The longer girl holds icicle, the more icicle melts/is not icicle.

There's an odd feeling of something huge and unethical growing inside you.
No two bit employment is acceptable, only this profitless past time,
hewing the anvil till split to the base, then building up something new

To work on next. Not the worship of frozen idols.Not gods of labor
and belief and the attendant process of dividing property, that wildly seething power
at the foundation of all which you pretend to have broken with too.

Sometimes in spring I linger for hours over the impression some idea or word
like "ice" has had on me, as if it were part of the voice of a fable
that was very nearly divine, veiled from view, far off, but not deep down

Only slightly lower than my head as it rests in my hands,
perhaps emanating from a source adjacent to my knees, opining endlessly
with the force of an earth shattering attachment, or perhaps a tune in the boughs

Yielding to a skyline adumbrated by the possibility of total loss.
Yes, its a voice near the knees making me smile the way the wind smiles,
widely, sail catching a good tail wind, tacking away from loss,

A sound like the wind possibly, sighing at what is significant
as one smiles after uncertainty, that rushing of wind nobody can touch or say,
some such sound as wind sounds lost from branch to branch

Because these linguistic tangents function as transducers,
transmitting power from one system to another,
retarding the impulse of time to finish its work and be done with it.

III

A sorceress waits inside her house, surrounded by the dubious tools of her trade.
Her inner plight resembles mine, vipers flailing about inside a pail.
For important journeys remember to pack your conceptual mythology.

From one end of the frozen skyline to the other — bulbs shining
inside glass towers — spiritual bodies reveal themselves to unscripted sense.
The weather comes up arctic again, dogs barking at someplace else

Nature a force that imagines us as empty as itself, dripping with
unrecognizable sadness still further inward, which bourgeois art also recognizes.
Grace of the partial thaw in the material substratum a fjord yawns in my tongue.

So too the freedom of the subject, which these dialings are designed to regurgitate.
Perhaps it released some secret anger in me. At the far end of the cafeteria
he nodded his head vigorously to communicate his delight at the news.

Because our material substratum remains liberty
so too the transcendental subject, which all digression is designed to rescue
from the latest tragic extreme, which is sovereign and has the last word

Charges out across the fjord in a frantic blaze, the last one awake.
All this strikes me as absurd today, and sad. Like a fawn that will not survive
even though it nibbles utopian fruit. As if I no longer possessed a luminous nature.

But I do. Or at least an anxious desire to join liquid and frozen into a single
twisting trail as when emotion and knowledge have both become adventure,
a something that circulates in the reckless mystery of what has not yet happened.

And it becomes imperative to sense echoes of a quite different meaning
incompatible with this one. As if we only learn the real name
if we renounce all other names by plumbing the real one through and through

So that in the end, obviously, I obtain none of the treasure — the monster still
guards the hoard — because I choose to continue to participate in the enchanting agony
of multiplicity. Through the half-open door, say, I see the table laid for breakfast.

"It's going to be hot out there today," my mother says, "a real scorcher."
Is this backward reference going to be prolonged to infinity or is there a final term
in secret parts, a skinned goat lolling white over the butcher's blue shoulder?

The "I" in the poem, reposing in a ground of unknown causes, is such a shell
abandoned by its muscle, though all its whorls and colors are still intact, a whole
subject to the selection of she who wades near shore and then returns to her blanket.

The reader who does not see this has not yet achieved
a total consonance between his inner and outer activity
and as such remains a nervous system and can be successfully interrupted.

And so on, all up in smoke, because these linguistic tangents function
as transducers, transmitting power from one system to another,
retarding the impulse of narrative to finish its work and be done with it.

Thanks to the material substratum remaining just as you have seen above
I hear a voice that is mine, and then another voice, that is not.
The girl was so enthusiastic about it that I was touched.

IV

What does it feel like to experience the mind in detachment
from the next black bird over that also knows how to float?
Writing opens us up to a fawn for whom the affirmative remains
                                        a basic nutritive need,

Reveals a brain capable of organizing a field of intelligible sleep objects
the skin and supporting bones of which have all but disappeared via benign neglect,
leaving behind a swirling texture constructed from incomprehensible
                                        dictums and signs.

If not, your material anger will fail to realize its transcendental possibilities
and the freedom of the subject, which this device fails to rescue,
will diffuse back into a hostile embassy, where it will surely be bugged.

After all it sometimes happens that the emotional foundation is less stable
than that pivot which allows us to inhale and exhale as we approach the peak
but that this non-reifiable remnant, due to the rocky labyrinths of the approach

Finally isn't worth the trouble, should instead have been expressed in utmost
Succinctness, through a systematic stripping down process or in terms of a loving
admonition of the experienced to the inexperienced to retain
                                        the subject's "freedom."

I set out in the morning and am back by the night.
At the base of the lighthouse I find you wiggling in a puddle of light.
I cannot see any difference between a porridge and a poem.

So too the secular tiling detaches itself from its grout and establishes
its own special homily to perfected realism, inside this frozen
part of speech, each *siecle d'or* overcome by its own uselessness.

But a contradiction in thought can be wholly creative too,
all allowances being made for the additional wear and tear to the psyche.
The eye that blends with the budding of an elm but maintains its brow

As a cocoon of thought so utterly fails to do when it bursts into action,
from above the moon to below the squid, psyche and budding elm,
unzipped self-estrangement creative of recognition or even the uncanny.

So I love you from the heart and cut you your first bits of meat
because language and the process of reification are interlocked
and people are spiders that we may never depart,

The inverse of a wall dividing one room from another,
what must melt like ice in order to create a desirable commonweal
from which to ascend to that fire in the air that can't ever be put out.

Yesterday one of the neighborhood children came here to play
and ended up nurturing in myself that bird with double vision,
the sorghum crop oh so close to its penultimate yearly harvest.

How think in terms of polyphonic stuff when in fact I only have one voice
which lies beneath and supports my oh so private voice, as in
                              the assigning of ministers
of outside and inside to this world of prose and seashells awed at being singled out.

Rather, lie awake, the poet said, sleep is confusion, the listing lids of inconsideration,
we may not be seeing each other again anyhow, "freedom" and its draped robes
never to be duplicated or taken for granted, unlike the prints on pajamas.

They lay there sleeping, sleeping and not sleeping, listening and not listening,
as if it were going to remain winter for an absurdly long time,
supposedly in connection with the girls not seeing each other again.

Being swallowed up and made perfect in the love of others
whose inner plight resembles yours, these world-shaking buds
yearning to reach the artistically necessary within an artistically impossible:

That words become the consciousness of an event,
not so much censor or witness as taggant
to an explosion whose source might otherwise remain a secret.

V

A sorceress waits inside her house, surrounded by the dubious tools of her trade.
I arrange my camera, admiring as always only my own adroitness,
and that rapidity with which I shuffle new ministers from cabinet to cabinet.

I set out in the in the morning and am back by the night.
In the time it takes to transcribe a phrase on behalf of another.
If, as she says, it is always best to start at the beginning, then this is the place.

All these traffic signals are indeed traffic signals, even the rocks,
                                    a non-reifiable remnant
slipping hieroglyphically between the meshes of a garrulous net,
saturated with substance and with the experience of the mind's own solitude.

Because these linguistic tangents function as transducers,
not as a downcast "no way" nobody can transmit from,
so too to add something on to the end of what has already been stated

Allows us to evade and thus curtail all the dragnets set for our identity.
True, our wallets have already been all but pilfered via forced entries
and more permanent embellishments, just as we reload the packhorse.

All these imitations are indeed imitations, even the roe, like an elegant remora
sucking insistently on the flanks of a Hollywood shark, saturated in death
and in the mind's mesmerism over the issue of its own possible digestion.

Such was my company during those seemingly mute days.
For we are all housed separately now, each in our own apartment.
This kind of deluded identity is the essence of ideology.

Not so! Under an alien sky wrecked sounds rack the waters.
We sailed on, in shock; a face appeared, moon-near, like ours.
Imagining blasted roads in a ruined country, a thing that once was prayed to

Flows down the dead mountains, mountain breathing in far mist.
There, under an alien sky, I had hoped to open a filling station.
As even a mediocre pianist will adjust the piano stool before he plays

I yowled down empty hallways, a wrenching sound that revives a memory,
a thing that once was prayed to. Fill the distances, like us, with what?
Deaf and blind, like the worms. As we wriggle onto this path of prose

Which is quickly followed by a crossroads
where "stupor" and "stupid" meet, the latter of which
is a route lined with signs and billboards and exit ramps into sullen towns

Twitching with impatience at their own patience.
As our ability to think transforms into our will to stop,
a sound that hums, wails, and then turns itself off

Not at the behest of the key in the ignition
but on the browned back of implications too painful to withstand
which no device you've yet thought of will be able to rescue

Or put in reverse. As if to have chosen Stupor, Amazement's sister,
over "stupid," which is just stupid, might have led to another outcome.
I set out in the morning and as I've already told you I'm back by the night

And always in the time it takes to admire my own adroitness.
Fortunately there was a sound on the train no one could pinpoint
and that remained untranslated, inexpressibly strange and nearly delightful

Except that it was also lulling in its unique montony, the rolling of waves
that only a cylinder plunging through darkness can conjure out of nothing
as it takes its leisure along the placid coast, senselessness burbling at its edges.

Just then our mighty vessel caught a good tail wind.
We sailed on in shock, our diamonds spilling overboard in the violence
of that gale, liberated from stones we had originally looted.

From one end of the carbonated shore to the other
I dreamt of opening a chain of filling stations under the sign of that other lute.
But we are all housed separately now, each in our own compartment.

As a child, car-bound, I stared at the back of a head for hours
passing through dark fires, swallowed up and perfected in the love of others
not so much as censor or witness as taggant inside the nuclear family.

Of the opposite of vision, within or outside of the language of daily life,
the other who speaks so precisely does not give him over into our hands
and, accordingly, always retains the freedom to lie.

    VI

Things had been going fine up till then.
A boarded up theater front suited our purposes perfectly.
A bathrobe pulled tight around my contours during the pupa stage

Language that was true to the experience of language, ever since that first moment
one was able to unbosom oneself in a new, half-realized tongue
richly tinged by tributary brooks and streams and sacrifices to the proscenium god

When suddenly this rapturous silence capsized into cacophony,
crackling admonitions of experience to inexperience, clouds draining
the insides of buildings whose material substratum remains substandard.

What of the old woman arguing with herself in the kitchen?
It sometimes happens that two people grow unconscious of each other
and the force of their contestation takes them into a veritable Hades

With the force of an earth shattering attachment, a drumming in the boughs
by which one's surviving personality is escorted to that land reserved for the dead,
no longer prisoner to its own dull instincts but rather to its choice of a beloved.

It sometimes happens too that two people grow conscious of each other
as hallucinated objects of failed wish fulfillment, each one on the verge of
coalescing into some kind of rational form for the other without
                                            ever quite managing it.

Now I am a radio, able to air myself in that new, half-realized frequency
with which radios will speak to anyone who will listen,
and capable of organizing new fields of sleep objects intelligible to millions.

You define animals as vague machines since you see with the eyes
of the manufacturing period, while before animals were our trusted aids.
They lay in their sheds sleeping, sleeping and not sleeping.

You define animals as vestigial machines, since you see with the eyes
of a transcendental technology, however much you strain to catch
the sound of some secret melody, materialized in memory.

Sinking into the sofa, as into a fish tank, you define a radio as a nonessential object
since you see with eyes that are now my essential fault, the ones that lead to
a tragic outcome, an outrage of the foreground against the background,

Background against the necktie, where intonation negates the message.
Actually I cannot be said to belong to either of the two because I cannot be
cut into pieces, but we will never get entirely behind our covert intentions

And into the sounding of that fjord, instead transgressing only what is necessary,
transmitting power from one system to another without retaining any ourselves.
Being cut to pieces should take us to a higher moral ground, but it doesn't.

To build is to collaborate with the earth, as amongst those who are animated
by translation as a form of ethics, never corroborated by anything but intuition.
The coughing abated after a few days. The sofa grew unnecessary.

        VII

Since the voice of the fable under construction contains something almost divine
the water in the water tower grows slightly restless, then warms to its task
and almost speaks and is about to speak and then forgets itself.

Suppose that each of your pondered instants could become nouns,
adjectives, adverbs, converted into verbs and stretching to communicate
extraordinary states of being after your thought had reached an impasse.

Sometimes I linger for hours over the impression some idea or word
has had on me, like the earth, after treatment with a tool
(penis symbol) that then is in position to bare fruit and pretty soon will,

However irritably. Verbal disagreements deal out specific hurts,
themselves the spawn of previous such fracas', utterly forgotten.
The one you want to see is much further on, she is still irritable.

Who often succeeds in going on only by banishing the wish from his consciousness.
We see the city piece by piece, digital clock/floating over/shipyard.
Parted water reunites behind our backs, "year three" as beautiful as molten gold

Yet cool, cool to the touch, and painted like sun flowers
by you know whom, of which I once had an actual experience.
Activities appropriate to paradisiacal condition, heart not under surveillance

Yet teeming with terrible textual errors that subsequently fuel
the refusal of direct satisfaction, the further refusal to accept that refusal,
one's wish rotating off the way the sun departs and evening comes

Heaven so near the objects we balk at, passionate constructions no two people
could ever dream in tandem, these little temporalities built on the browned back
of implications too painful to withstand, just as we reload the stubborn donkey.

Faces turn like planets around a fixed star and in turning they constantly turn away.
I don't need a program to understand what is happening in this elemental space.
We have begun to say goodbye to each other and cannot say so.

Nothing is gained by whining about the soulessness of the sea anemone
that the other has dared to conceive of as dreaming of something
as it filters water through its body in the momentum and wash of the ill-defined —

A broken windowpane just as good as a quivering mouth, a heap of half-smoked
steaming cigarettes serves as well as the nervous drumming of fingers,
not because either of these are clever or soulful, but because each is also ill-defined —

Just as a writer who uses an archaic form bathed in the preciousness of some
bygone era isn't by definition dim witted or of a pale cold light that was only once
alive. Such things just maybe belong to the moon we do not see

And form a complex background of shifting lights and shadows,
curtains, smoke, and sordid fripperies, hints rather than states, hoof marks of
which are bronzed on the flowing mountains in repetitive zigzag motives.

What I wanted more than anything else was to become rooted in another land.
When contemplating migration it is important to pack a mythic self.
Suddenly the poem came as if a coda, a hand of light at the lip of the dolmen.

Eating, sleeping, reading, working: warming oneself in luminous rays.
Rapture begins with the annihilation of the immediate, before the world
gets its chance to fix us as bodies, objects, commodities.

I set out from the morose and get as far as the nimble, the tongue taking on
the task of transcribing the nether world. Sorghum waits patiently
                                              to ripen to maturity
surrounded by the teeth that traditionally chew it; trees must again be trees.

Perhaps all this revives itself in rapidly melting ice, one end of the imagination
a blinking arrow pointed towards an indoor parking lot, half the time happily
obscuring the view, the other half not, as if to apologize for still being present.

Designed by Samuel Retsov

੨ৡ

Text: 11 pt Janson

੨ৡ

Printed on acid-free paper

੨ৡ

Printed by McNaughton and Gunn